A NOWHERE FOR VALLEJO

Shearsman Library Vol. 18

BOOKS BY NATHANIEL TARN

POETRY

Old Savage/Young City (1964) / *Where Babylon Ends* (1969)
The Beautiful Contradictions (1969; 2nd edition 2013)
October (1969) / *The Silence* (1969)
A Nowhere for Vallejo (1971 (USA), 1972 (UK); 3rd edition 2023*)
Section: The Artemision (1973)
The Persephones (1974; revised editions, 2008, 2016)
Lyrics for the Bride of God (1975)
The House of Leaves (1976; 2nd edition 2018*) / *The Microcosm* (1977)
Atitlán / Alashka [*Alashka* with Janet Rodney] (1979)
Weekends in Mexico (1982) / *The Desert Mothers* (1984; 2nd edition 2018*)
At the Western Gates (1985; 2nd edition 2018*)
Palenque: Selected Poems 1972–1984 (1986*; 2nd edition 2023*)
Seeing America First (1989) / *Home One* (1990)
The Army Has Announced that Body Bags… (1992)
Caja del Río (1993) / *Flying the Body* (1993) / *The Architextures* (2000)
Three Letters from the City: The St. Petersburg Poems (2001)
Selected Poems: 1950–2000 (2002) / *Recollections of Being* (2004)
Avia (2008*) / *Ins & Outs of the Forest Rivers* (2008) / *Gondwana* (2017)
Alashka [with Janet Rodney] (first separate publication, 2018*)
The Hölderliniae (2021)

TRANSLATIONS

Pablo Neruda: *The Heights of Macchu Picchu* (1966)
Pablo Neruda: *Selected Poems* (1968) / Victor Segalen: *Stelae* (1969)
Con Cuba (1969) / The Rabinal Achi, Act 4 (1973)
The Penguin Neruda (1975) / Jean-Paul Auxémery: *Selected Poems* (2021)

PROSE

Views from the Weaving Mountain:
Selected Essays in Poetics & Anthropology (1991)
Scandals in the House of Birds: Shamans & Priests on Lake Atitlán (1998)
The Embattled Lyric: Essays & Conversations in Poetics & Anthropology (2007)
Atlantis: An Autoanthropology (2021)

* from Shearsman Books

Nathaniel Tarn

A NOWHERE FOR VALLEJO

CHOICES

OCTOBER

Shearsman Library

Second British Edition.
Published in the United Kingdom in 2023 by
The Shearsman Library
an imprint of Shearsman Books
PO Box 4239
Swindon
SN3 9FN

Shearsman Books Ltd Registered Office
30–31 St. James Place, Mangotsfield, Bristol BS16 9JB
(this address not for correspondence)

www.shearsman.com

ISBN 978-1-84861-904-3

*First published by Random House, New York in 1971,
and Jonathan Cape, London, in 1972.*

South

Contents

I.

A NOWHERE FOR VALLEJO

"Y madrugar, poeta, nómada,
al crudísimo día de ser hombre"

"Yo vine a darme lo que acaso estuvo
asignado para otro;"

LOS HERALDOS NEGROS

For a New Realism

"Verdejo, Castelo and Bastidas were hanged pure and simple. Francisco Túpac Amaru, uncle of the rebel, and Hipólito, his son, had their tongues cut out before being thrown from the steps of the gallows. The Indian girl Condemaita was garroted on an instrument with an iron winch, made for this purpose and never previously seen in these parts. The rebel and his wife, having witnessed these tortures – their son being the last to be taken to the gallows – Micaela, wife of the rebel, was taken to the apparatus, where, under her husband's eyes, she had her tongue cut out and was garroted – something which took a long time, for her neck was so delicate that they could not catch her in the instrument. The executioners had to tie her neck with ropes, push and pull her from each side, kicking her breast and belly, to finish her off. The rebel José Gabriel closed the proceedings and was taken to the center of the Plaza. There, the executioner cut his tongue out, took off fetters and handcuffs, tied four ropes to his hands and feet and secured the ropes to the harnesses of four horses which four mestizos led off in four different directions. This spectacle too had never been seen in this day. I do not know whether the horses were weak, or whether the Indian was made of iron, but they were completely unable to tear him to pieces. After pulling him about for a while—he being in the air like a spider – the Visitador, seized with compassion that this unfortunate suffer no more, sent an order from the Compañía, where he was directing the execution, that the executioner should cut his head off – which was duly done. The body was then taken to the gallows where arms and feet were cut off. The same was done to the wife; and the other victims' heads were cut off to be taken to various villages round about. The bodies of the Indian and his wife were taken to a bonfire at Picchu, where they were reduced to ashes, the ashes being thrown into the fields and a rivulet running nearby. In this manner ended José Gabriel Túpac Amaru and Micaela Bastidas, whose pride and arrogance had reached such heights that they styled themselves kings of Peru, Chile, Quito, Tucuman and other parts, unto the inclusion of the great Paitití, and other madnesses of this ilk.

A great crowd of people came on that day, but no one cried out or spoke out loud. Many people took notes, including myself, and were surprised to find that in such a crowd Indians were not to be seen, at least in their own costumes; and if there were any, they disguised themselves in capes and ponchos.

A number of things happened which look as if the Devil worked to confirm these Indians in their abuses, auguries and superstitions. I note it down, for in the midst of days beautifully dry and serene, this one turned out to be so overcast that the sun could not be seen and rain threatened from all quarters. And at twelve noon, when the horses were pulling the Indian, there came a great gust of wind, and after this a rain shower which made everyone, including the soldiers, run for cover at great speed. This is the reason Indians have begun to say that the sky and elements felt the death of the Inca that the Spaniards, inhuman and impious, were killing with such cruelty."

> *Eye-witness account of the execution in Cuzco on Friday, May 18, 1781, of the rebel José Gabriel Túpac Amaru, last descendant of the Royal Line, self-styled Inca of Peru, from a document in Boleslao Lewin: "La Insurrección de Túpac Amaru," Eudeba, Buenos Aires, 1963.*

A Nowhere for Vallejo

(A)

"Yo nací un día
que Dios estuvo enfermo,
grave."
LOS HERALDOS NEGROS

Conch shells at Mass
   alcaldes standing golden cloaks
staffs tipped with silver
   alpaca lining shield flocks on their knees

priest dropping shards for the thousandth time
   of shattered language
the sacristan distributes herbs of grace
   and lights to the village elders

as suddenly
    the church roof sails
        several feet into the air
the Sun opens its arms

the risen Host covers the face of the Sun like a kerchief
   and the wild thrones bellow
       dominations howl
archangels blare

      a poet born
from the depths of the sea
      in Santiago de Chuco
on the scar of Peru

and female the soul of the absent one
and female my very own
till when shall we be waiting for
what no one owes us

13

People at the door outside
        press in against the temple
cheeks to their fathers' stones
                cave in like the walls of the sea

Sad destiny not to have ever lived   but dead forever
        being dry leaf   unknown to green
            orphan of orphans
                    and
Mother   I go tomorrow to Santiago
           to wet me in your benedictions and your tears

A child of seven
        ravished by the fiesta procession
especially   the standard-bearer
        racing home to his mother

Mother   I want to be the standard-bearer

Conch shells at Mass
        alcaldes gathered at the door
shrunk in the light of flash-bulbs
        a girl throwing petals on the vicar's head   he shrugs them off

I shall come back to Peru when not one stone is left standing

I.

*"Tal la tierra oirá en tu silenciar,
cómo nos van cobrando todos
el alquiler del mundo donde nos dejas
y el valor de aquel pan inacabable."*
                                    TRILCE

And they went down into the king-city
Tahuantinsuyu   four-quarters   limbs of man
                              to find the skull

happening there   first thing   on the poet's name
who'd become such a hero to his country
                    though he had left it
they'd finally put up a statue in the square
                    fronting the church of famine

and he walked up to the monument
                    and kissed the poet's name
with his hand

In "La Langouste Selon Désir"
he heard the wind going through her tears
the bird feeds its young in the myth
opened its breast   blood flowing out
                    flapped lazily over city and harbour
catch of fish   dying children

Bird-glider over the city
wall-wings / oven-beak
falls on the statue of the caesar-poet
                    bread on the sea

Where they buy and sell a country
                    we were talking about the dead with the rich
eating their platos criollos
                    in "The House of the Thirty Coins"

talking with the satellite vendors
                with which the country we don't know
listens to the one we do

In a city full of movement
with the woman he loves
crying for the caesar-poet to come back
                and eat them alive one by one
the friends   the enemies
                                eat them all
in words born and dead at this table

and then a constant
     quiet
murmur about gold

he hears the wind going through her tears
her tears   the queen-city
married a king with her hair in his eyes
above the grave of the caesar-poet

he feeds the children crying in her tears

II.

"Es el tiempo este anuncio de gran zapatería
es el tiempo, que marcha descalzo
de la muerte   hacia   la muerte?
POEMAS HUMANOS

Call of green things to his hand
         no longer pulls
underworld gold
         pales for his lack of envy

The things of poverty
         he sees as clear
as mountain teeth
         about to bite the sky
as the backbone of mountains
         about to puncture the sky's belly

The city is grey with white hands
         the city
                        the city
is grey with white   and green   hands
         beckons the forests
cold mountain's reaches

They say the same mists will come down
         but be drunk by the Sun
they say there will be a Sun up there
         but it will be cold

Old man in a brown hat
         drip at his nose
passing
         the eyes   /   of a door through mountains
one way
         with no thought of return

Frozen to gold
        demonetized gold
to be dug up at dawn
        changed into mountains
glass-enclosed
        changed into mountains

Wind on the sands   cat-god   mouse
        mouse on cat   cat on mouse
lovers lying side by side in the mountains
                        he is about to enter

Her oyster is the Moon's
        around it   a city
prayer in his hands
        calls to the caesar-poet

                        venture out there

And where are you
                macho
in all this sleep
        rotting about our bodies

Taken a bus twice only   these fifteen years

III.

"Y preguntamos por el eterno amor,
por el encuentro absoluto,
por cuanto pasa de aquí para allá."
TRILCE

In the Andean night
he saw her shed ha skin and come out of herself
        as from a chrysalis   the walls of cunning
and she stood up inside herself

a moth enjoying the wind

Her right hand went out   bearing an offering
her left hand also   at about the same height
        they took her for Justice discussing this country
night broke the balance   her feathered mouth

brushing their genitals   man after man

and those who had etched their names on her walls
a death's-head now   between her shoulder-blades
        fell   powder from her wings
onto the highroads of the continent

moth-dust on rolling tires

Ageing priest on the plaza
dressed in the flesh she had worn before birth
        flayed god of sacrifice
dances   her pores will want to speak

and the people back away like Spring rain

He knows where she has lost the thread
of the myth they constructed together
        yet their life opens on down
she has no means of ever closing it

19

He said   he said   in the rush of air
        as sand blew in the maze
as the labyrinth silted up

                        that desert's name

IV.

*"Yace la cuerda así al pie del violín
cuando hablaron del aire, a voces, cuando
hablaron muy despacio del relámpago."*
POEMAS HUMANOS

Friar   leans forward   talks to empty air
      they follow in his wake
dawn switched on silver treasures
      Beethoven dawns with light   later   some Strauss

Monstrance with a shining gaze
      the woman's eye   asleep in his dreams
the girl with eyelashes of Sun
      bedded in the king-city

Rose of the city
      crowned by the Jesus-Child
small lover in her arms   her white-black robe
      the sweetest rose that Jesus ever blew

Boats in the streets as they leave
      the black saint with his broom against her spine
his dog his dove his cat his mice
      and the fish-wind off Callao

Where sea and Sun are woven
      with the rusting veins of the mountains
the speech-gods   as she stretches out
      long scrolls of roses on their lips

the silver heart   gracias a Dios
      the broom sweeping the mountains
a condor-fan   the whole spread bird
      and rattles in the beads of corn

Sailing the streets as they leave
      wind racing in the dark over sands
bones in the catacombs
      pegged to the wall in ornamental scrolls

sting-ray with a human face
      floating towards the mountains
tame pelicans in the market place
      sociedad de amigos del pescado

and the fish-wind   having no name
      vandal bees at their honey
having no gift of sleep   therefore no name
      the holy rose has flown beyond

no longer broods   Rimac   the speaker's bones

V.

"Ah, mujer! Por ti existe
la carne hecha de instinto."
LOS HERALDOS NEGROS

They met the sex-god on the road
with oily muscles   sweat in the small of his back
                              she said
turn your back to me
                              he said
no   yours to me
                              they never knew which side he came
he left that day   never came back

loping towards the mountains
                         the exercise is good   he said
never stop spending on this road
                         all envy will desist

She nursed an eagle
seemed to them
but could have been
                         most any other bird
both with their eyes downcast
and so tender an embrace in the middle of all the fucking
                         it could have been that swan-girl
(in tender mood)   and in another country

while they tried every sin in the manual
                         on all those pots
fellatio
      much sodomy
                    the dog positions
some gaped like cunts
                  some wept on stalks
but the bird-couple crouched   locked in each other's wings

The frozen sand
glaciers of sand   oils drained to sea
pop ads in small black cactus
                    pinned to the sand by the road-makers
between the gringo ads
the names of all our loves
                    miguel   carmencita   miguel
and   No Hay Justicia

A lorry   The Seven Tongues   going north
I Go with God   a lorry   going south
A lorry   Star of Trujillo   going north
No Hay Amor   a lorry   going south

They passed the sex-god on the road
driving towards the mountains
                    the sweat a crust on his back
the green banana slung between his legs

(B)

"El valle es de oro amargo;
y el viaje es triste, es largo."
LOS HERALDOS NEGROS

From mountains   in his eighteenth year
       to cloistered city   sea among its walls
initiated study   body   spirit
       about the time of Spring   about the resurrection
dropped out because of penury
       teaching the young what he had never learned
mid-year a time for travels
       the Fall   for action

Young well-to-do
       guns   hounds   and fighting cocks
closing their houses to all but the sea
       girls fall to pass his watches
a yellow billet in his yellow hands
       his verses made   out of the medievals
his spirit-kin   Rimbaud   the other French
       even in prison   prizes   competitions

And we would see him crossing
       the ficus-shaded streets
locked behind doors   washed in our rooms
       on our own solitudes
his garments black   a lion's mane
       black lion's mane   from cordilleras
always his elegance   each day a dandy
       his clothes with little work to do   upon those bones

Trujillo-Lima   elegant boats
       cold captains giving orders
I'll be the one who's gone
       until the boat for France   El Oroyo   third class
in a sad mid-June   where he would never rest
       before he'd died of Spain   like Garcilaso

Peruvian tongue   choked in its walls
        scum on colonial tides

And his loves   shut oysters
        betrayed to knives   numbered   outnumbered
love-speech to the roses of the coastal cities
        awash on sleep   the sleep of childhood
What are you doing now   my sweet   my andine Rita
        of rushes   of capuli
her sex   a tomb   shut to the sea at last
        calls him in from the streets

After the fire   that night of chichas
        Darío singing   *las Américas celestes*
they were all of one mind to arrest him
        wherever found   for a dubious crime
the court long closed in that Pacific province
        far   dying star of his youth
would harrow   extradite   imprison him   in dreams
        even in the city of light

They have taken a poet prisoner   Doctor Polar
        imagine   a poet prisoner
But that is inconceivable   Who is the poet
        The great poet Vallejo   Doctor Polar

Gravest time of my life   in a Peruvian jail

VI.

"Father Condor, take me,
Brother Falcon, take me,
Tell my little mother I am coming,
For five days I have not eaten, or drunk a drop,
Father messenger, bearer of signs, swift messenger,
Carry me off, I beg you: little mouth, little heart,
Tell my little father and my little mother, I beg you,
that I am coming"

QUECHUA POEM

Mountains at the feet of mountain
        cradled in fire
mountains behind mountains
          reaching towards the cold
mountains handing each other up
               like generations

crops   cape of feathers
        on the ancestor's shoulders
and blue the lupin in the wind
          scarlet the tanager
               the swallow-hawk

black   over all

Mountains inside of mountains
fields   ringed   smoking prayers
mountains presented
        on palms of other mountains
white clouds
            their shirts of snow

sky-sucked   snow udders
he suckles in his sleep
helmets of snow
        on his skull of rock
fists of snow in her mouth
          uncurls and sucks their fingers

Below the blue   a swatch of chocolate
grey lava   mountain-tears
green copper   peat   lichen   moss
                white droppings of the falcon
his rainbow shoots her up
                                    to suck the stars

and the crops of soft cloth on the wind
woven of feathers and hair
gold-plated mantle   kerchief dry in the Sun
                these treasures on his shoulders
the caesar-poet
                            clothed in his mountains

Sickle of skirts   rims of blood
shearing the mountains
with his head in the clouds
                he speaks to her sex
parting the pubis
                            wears her crops like a beard

looks down from the top of the world
        and
            falls
        slow
            cataract
                    of
                    land
into Huaráz

VII.

"Calor, cansado voy con mi oro, a donde
acaba mi enemigo de quererme."
POEMAS HUMANOS

Word of thin gold
        letting them in
letting them out
        the imprisoned hand
is the hand set free
        the hand setting free
is the hand that locks

and the heart
        that he could not enter
and the eyes   behind their gates
        and the mind he could not read
locked in gold-leaf
        his needle to
the death of love

They sank the golden rod
        at Huanacauri   sank first time
clothed like the Sun in his clothes
        went out   he north   she south
out of the inn of morning
        and they set up   pillars
wreathed in flowers and sweet herbs
        for the Sun to come and sit on
in all its light

Through the high plateau
        wind moved on grass
one horseman   a statue
        far from his sheep
another one
        surrounded by his sheep
a knife in butter

Chaotic range   white belt of mountains
                    horizon snow
little balls of cloud
                    tossed by the gods at play

domes   minarets of cloud   for Garcilaso
                    in Córdoba de los Olivares
polo   among the singer-gods

and over all
                    Huascarán
the saddle-mountain
                    with the gods astride
their horse of snow
                    parading through their conquests
with sticks of light

In the quiet town
                    gold made / unmade
humming bird to his tasks
                    flighting atop his dance
putting in extras
                    some madness in the nectar
describing curlicues
          for morning's joy
                    in the arms of their father the Sun

VIII.

"En el muro de pie, pienso en las leyes
que la dicha y la angustia van trocando:"
LOS HERALDOS NEGROS

Borders slide backwards   forwards
weak kings   lose a strong king's conquests
            Sun-image on the mountain lakes
empire provider   whether cold or hot
                reigns from the start of time

His train   a messenger
agonizes between the mountains
                at loss for a breath of air
through eye of rock
                into the mountain's skull
forward   then back   forward then   back
                forward again
locates a stream of air
                hardly dares breathe it

At four thousand five hundred   climbing
                passes out of earth's hold
out of its grasp and keep
                spine   transparent now
    snake-vertebrae
                in a royal necklace
    eyes crystallized
                    gone beyond darkness
    on the edge of light
                lungs failing
sucking like bellows
                sight improving
all the time
                until at last he comes
a riveder le stelle

And he has seen
                gigantes / monstruos
teeth prison-bars
                gargantas   famine
dueños de los montes
                the archangelical
Michel et toute sa compagnie
                        du temps de sa jeunesse
in his day of youth

Where Justice goes   puffs along tracks
                with her dimmed eyes
breasts   flanks of mountains
                purse-bellied after many children
and cleft of earthquake

Sun astride mountains   mail of gold

IX.

"Pacífico inmóvil, vidrio, preñado
de todos los posibles.
Andes frío, inhumanable, puro.
Acaso. Acaso"

TRILCE

Rain coming down
    from a hurricane on the coast
blotting Sun from his mind
    drowning his ancestors
in a month he had never yet known

    Graves by the sea
tunnelled in sand
    mummies wrapped in rich cloth
hands raised to cheeks
    in gestures of horror
undressed by rain
    ropes slipping from them
the food pots filling up with water

On level beach
    cat-god and priests
in a foot of brine
    dance the dance of refreshment
and the stars over Paracas
    send long streamers down
on the midnight wind
    which has lost its mind

    Astride the cordillera
the caesar-poet
    washes golden garments
with an alpaca cloth
    Coya the beautiful
fulfills her pots with dew
    teaches her whistles
water-bird calls

Blotted out from their minds
    the north   the south
the high caminos to the provinces
    Sun-pillars drowned
water-clock flooded
    calendar gone beyond recall
and their defenses breached
    imperial walls

    Snakes in the water
their sinews dance
    the poet swims with Coya
in a passion of waters
    they clean their skins
ring out their hair
    sing to one another
the unrecorded songs

and the beautiful country
    and the marble stairs
and the Sun's pillar
    and the Moon's thighs
drink in the waters
    disappear without trace
until the Sun comes out
    preening bird   in his marvels

X.

"ante el pesar de los padres de no poder dejarnos
de arrancar de sus sueños de amor a este mundo;"
                                    TRILCE

Passing the Palace of Justice
        a taxi-driver says
great deal of palace
                for so little justice

Photographers in rain
        their cameras backed up
storks at the Station wall
        trapped in their own last portraits

Where they mine his ores
        wrecks of better housing
under crumbling mountains
                in the high towns
there are no gardens
        children tell homes apart
by numbers on the blocks
        Arbeit macht frei

Noses stuffed against dust
        on the prowl for their lungs
whole babies under shawls
        stifle in mother smell
while guts torn up
        golden wombs opened
give up their treasures
                puffing down to the coast

The wounded country
        whose past is drained
by vampire and vulture
        out of whose wounds

35

torrent of ore
      angry and sick
such men have drained
      to add their own blood to the torrent

And the caesar-poet
      walks in far Paris his night-walk
exhausted by Justice
        as he falls to his drink
cats lap the blood
      of the land he recovers in dreams

His fathers   from the hills
      look down erosion
try tracing paths
        messengers travelled
to bring news of the Sun
          bread to his children

    smouldering arms to the mines

(C)

"¡Haber nacido para vivir de nuestra muerte!
¡Leventarse del cielo hacia la tierra
por sus proprios desastres"

POEMAS HUMANOS

"Su cadáver estaba lleno de mundo."

ESPAÑA, APARTA DE MI ESTE CALIZ

Sharp cataract of rain
on Paris streets
dance   lights of cars
light gliding   mist and rain
backdrop of fog
ballerina rain-drops
on his spirit's stage
gutters   from Amazons
to occidental Andes of eternity

Shall die in Paris   with the coming of showers
on a day I already remember

Town-light   town-smell
smell of light   drifting up from this place
claw-hands   money-hands
beggars with crying hands
weeping fingers
mouths like the morning star
before he chokes
a woman's yes   with her dying breath
he trembles for the race

Shall die in Paris   with the coming of showers

Metro
cinquante centimes
till one a.m.   closing time

37

wanders bowels of Paris
where roots drink sea
explores his country's mines
among silent roots
then cut   to star watch
benches and batons

Shall die in Paris   with the coming of showers

Running
pawnshop to pawnshop
never getting enough
holy chair   holy table
Beethoven's head
proceeds lost on getting there
paying various taxes
rips   tramites   taxis
dregs gobbled in some good restaurant

Shall die in Paris   with the coming of showers

Saved   little foxes   saved at last
ourselves   our little vixens
 belly first   *zorillos míos*
La politique est un art aussi   Madame
who saved the lining of his pants
standing   wherever travelled
shoes   not getting off the metro
until it stopped completely
you'll learn to tame in time   your sporting instincts

Shall die in Paris   with the coming of showers

Stir punch
dance round   the alta sierra punch
throw lemons   bitter herbs
more wine   more sugar

never talk poetry   never read poems
sing   *At the river Huanchaca*
shall throw myself in
no one to see or feel
or have knowledge of love

Shall die in Paris   with the coming of showers

Pass through men   through women
through the city of light
not bohemian by nature
misery hurts a great deal
no fiesta for me
as it is for some others
humblest tramp has travel
wires trembling over seas
Only this Indian stays   at the edge of the feast

Shall die in Paris   with the coming of showers
                        on a day I already remember

Going to Spain
going to Santiago to see my mother
going to Spain
magi   magicians   magnetizers
work round the death bed
tiring him further
                        and they puncture his lungs
but receive no liquid
veins turned to gold
changed   into mountains

Play me   he said   *a little Beethoven*
he had   like that   some bourgeois ways

XI.

"And particularly as regards the City of Cuzco, which
was my mother, and mistress of this Empire, I feel
that I must keep it from falling into oblivion
GARCILASO DE LA VEGA, EL INCA

The earth they tower over
    as far above cloud
as clouds are from the ground
    unveiled at once
grasped as a whole
    with its cheeks of water

Yet those-who-see-everything
    have not touched the limits yet
delved into every valley
    not carried roads as far as they will go
blue lungs inhaling on the western ocean
    green snakes   equatorian rivers
toy herds paralysed in their fields
    rain-forest east   the blow-pipe people
border lake in the south

and the Sun-city   in its shawl of hills
    altars of gold and glass
the harp   a heart with its music
    for the dead in their coffins of stone
markets smothered in cloth
    threads groping out to the hills
to the flanks of the sneering alpaca
    the beasts circling round the city
homing   on the four roads

and grease to the Lord of Earthquakes
    two hearts in the umbilical city
Garcilaso the Inca in his palace
    dreaming old vassaldoms

on his mother's lips
    to spell in Arab Córdoba
the hunchback lunatic in La Merced
    he who knows not Cuzco knows not Peru
and it enters into you   almost always   by way of surprise

The caesar-poet
    asleep in the city
leaves of fire in his mouth
    crowned with his thorns
waits out his return   to Santiago de Chuco
    beyond Pisac   beyond Colla
dreams in Plaza de Armas   Cathedral gold
    with bride   half-sister
Sun-child   among his weapons

To the holy world
    laws to be given at last
prepared for their appointed time
    dormant until required
each day   he gives his light and brilliance
    goes round the world each day
to gain a better knowledge of the people's needs
    to satisfy these needs   follow that track
        you'll draw each being to you   only by love

XII.

"¡Yo que tan sólo he nacido!"

"En suma no poseo para expresar mi vida sino mi muerte."
POEMAS HUMANOS

"Ángela, yo siempre he llegado tarde."
VALLEJO TO ÁNGELA RAMOS

Brought here in spirit
    to be given life
where peaks out-tower the sun
    brought here in body
to have life taken away
    where the meaning of height is made clear
heart torn out in sacrifice
    by the beautiful lady of death
where the meaning of height is made clear

    Not been through here
        never touched   this nowhere
    these hills
        nor trod these valleys
    where the meaning of height is made clear
        not gone through passages
    between valley and hill
        not been changed into valleys
    changed into mountains

These peaks at the heart are well-known
    their shapes recorded
but the quality of dying here is different
    he writes at the gates   while his life bleeds
writes before knowledge
    going into the altars
where his death is laid out
    remembering their joys
set out as they are   in his recorded songs

He knows her talk
        it is the talk of a woman leaving a man
to go to another
        or to set out   into uncovered solitude
from which she will not issue
        sworn virgin to the Sun
but that man   he too is picked by death
        but that solitude   it too is gravelled by death
in death's own hour

Eyes dry beyond tears
        he quotes her lines he has written for her
shaped from the stones of her sides
        for in the poem   they have not lived in time
they have not lost their vantage on eternity
        and known no longer   whether she is of day
night   life   or death
        he has decided   to be her poet all his life
by straight subscription

        But she has gone down for the life of day
            caress of butterflies
        kindness of birds
            she has decided against eternity
        for the touch of fish
            or an animal's tongue
        and the weight of a man is no longer agreeable to her
            her star has festered from the start
        while he has been turning the world

The distances
        she has preserved all this time
death-tick of watches
        now measure stone   snake-skin
rare orchid blossom
        and he writes
to preserve her life

to seal her liberty
to encourage her lovers

His image of her
writhing in her own hands
on her own   in the dark
who can tell anymore
among these mountains
the peak of her especial spirit
she has become
while he has turned the world
a terrible star

And of her going
melting away
assuming new shapes
fitting herself to other bodies
of her fresh interests   in the cause of other loves
her departures   her arrivals
unknown to him in the night
there is no more end
than there is to mountains

She walks through sleep
as he lies on his side
along the city walls   where all roads lead
moves like a swimmer
across stone windows
and the doubts in his eyes
between his eyelids she has gone as far as she dares
like a kite   never frees him entirely
he faints   the first time in his life

Accepting nothing
cloth   silver   pictures   beads
no memory of time among the dry ruins
he becomes the past.

suddenly   he becomes the past
        her eyes shine with a peaceful future
she has gone from the land of the dead
        where he was not in their time
he is there now

        And he'll forget
            then forget to forget
        the world will end
            he is not its master
        whatever he thinks of the matter
            to whatever extent he can explain
        or not explain
            quite apart from him   in its own crucibles
        the world will come to an end

For it could have been anyone
        almost any one at all
love chose to put her in his way
        made her his target
the beautiful lady of death
        but what made love go as far as that
rather than pick out another
        time behind time   mountain behind mountain
no longer knows   no longer cares

        And love was like a god in the heart
            wrenching this way and that
        having his way
            he was aware of her   of her beautiful hands
        while the mountains tumbled
            her touch of fingers on his sleep
        more in his pain   perhaps
            more through her tears
        than ever in the flower of their days

And she thanked him for the wonderful day
       at the end of the day
as he thanked her
       the day he'd come to die
and his fist had unclenched
       nail-heads reaching the palms
at noon of night
       letting her drop
out of grasp   out of hold

    Now he braces himself

    never to hate the world

    for having lost her

XIII.

*"Llegué a confundirme con ella,
tanto…!"*

LOS HERALDOS NEGROS

At Intihuatana
    hitching post of the Sun
in grief's wonderful fire
    he gathered himself into himself
Coya beside him
    made custom to the lords of the place

The gladiolus in its mindful blaze
    orchids in purple mantles
maidenhair ferns in their quivers
    arrowheads of bamboo
black antlers from the burning fields
    eyelids of passing clouds

rose up to Intihuatana
    and the art of stone   the art of drains
the art of steps   the art of terraces
    the art of corners   the art of chinks
the art of doors   the art of lintels
    came to groan at the feet of the Sun

Boulders in situ
    related aptly   to what is built upon them
this secret of the city
    gathered into his feet
walks to the monument   the gate of time
and kisses the Sun   with his hand

calls fathers   mothers
    in threadbare blankets
begging pardon for molestia
    winds   clouds   peaks   thunderbolts

hair and lashes of rain
    all he knows   all he doesn't know

that there might be life for these servants
    that the door might be opened into the dark
the Moon illuminate her daughter's steps
    and the Sun the manner of her parting
that there might be peace in the dismembered heart
    and the ground-dove's voice be stilled

Dogs came to piss on the threshold of Intihuatana
    women profaned it with their feet
foreigners squinting through cameras
    lovers unaware of their noise
wrapped in the aura about the stone
    they were pure in his passion of stillness

and the gods responded with butterflies
    to dance their wedding dance
before him   before her   before her
    before both jointly   the single butterfly
after which came another of that species
    and they made off together on a sigh

and the gods confirmed their responses
    male hawk coming in over the city
to the stone where the female waited
    covered her in a trice   without much prelude
then dropped to meditate
    as she bore his seed away

XIV.

"Cállate. Nadie sabe que estás en mí,
toda entera. Cállate. No respires."

TRILCE

On the train to the ruins
as the mountains grew taller and taller
    until no one believed them
wrapped in himself   he cried behind his glasses
    his eyes two white moths
and she watched him   from behind her book
    grieving for him
        never moved forward

Had lain three days   face to the floor
    how sick she must have been
        of weeping men

and I speak for her   he thought
    since she has no mouth
    sleeps under dust   with all my dead

    Coming back from the ruins
    meaning of height made clear
    they touched each other's hands
    as each marvel appeared
    breasts of a Moon survivor
    hard nipples   bitter ink
    nestled in her white shirt
    brushing his cheek as they moved

A preacher at the back of the train
    was telling young men how to live
    whose eyes already knew

Gringas   in nearby seats
    a bitter tale of dollars
    things they had failed to buy

Eyes of puma   fox   llama
rushes lying down in the fire
          eyes of deer in evening sunshine
eyes of adobe huacos
          eyes in which corn has brewed
eyes of charcoal cinders
          eyes of alpaca wool in mist
          under the smoke of his hurt

We shall arrive by night   he thought
we shall arrive in the city by night
          the city we've not seen for some time
no one will know we've come
          we'll go about our dowry
our marvelous marriage-bed
          a little later yet
          be heard of elsewhere

(D)

I.

"Empiezo a reconocer en la suma miseria
mi vía autentica y única de existencia."
VALLEJO TO PABLO ABRIL, xii.xi.mcmxvii

In the same way   suffered most cautiously
thus not to cry or weep   since eyes themselves
have   independently of self   their poverties
*   I mean to say   their functions*
                                        something
that skids front soul   and falls to soul

          Orphan of language
          orphan of orphancies
          black debt in Paris
          disdain in Lima
          To do no more than die
          need death at every moment

Pablo   there are in life
hours of a black   closed blackness
shut to all consolation
*   hours more sinister   I'd say*
more awesome than the tomb

          I do not know
          the paths that lead to comfort
          to happiness
          have never taken them
          Thus all is well   very well as it is
          and above all   in essence

This child's facility for tears
sunk in huge pity for all things
remembering my fathers   often   dear ones lost

51

One day   I shall manage to die
in the hazardous life I've had to carry

and then   as now
you'll witness me
minus encouragement
or almost any love
I have no present
or for that matter   future

And if   after so many words
the word itself failed to survive
and if   after bird wings
the bird at rest   failed to survive
Better in truth   eat everything   and finish

And as for politics
I've gone according to
the proper weight of all things
Understand me Juan   one lives one's life
and it enters into him
almost always   by way of surprise

As I go on living
life teaching me
I am getting much clearer about ideas and feelings
relative to the matters and men of America
It seems to me   we need great fury
and a terrible destructive impulse for everything
to be found in those places
One must destroy   and destroy oneself
This can't go on   must not go on
Since we have no leaders to rely on
we must unite   at least   in a tight bundle
of wounded and furious people
burst out   tearing to pieces
all things around us   or in our power

Above all   we must destroy ourselves
and afterwards   the others
        Without the prior sacrifice of self
        there is no possible salvation

                Leaving les flics   in the andine air
                        of Paris town   the poet said
                We owe life nothing now
                        and have the right to be happy

Everything's happy   except my happiness

II

        "*And all the idols had remained unanimously silent*
                which filled the king with terror; he thought
                that the Sun itself must be in distress…"
                GARCILASO DE LA VEGA, EL INCA

So we might know
the enormous quantity of gold it takes to be poor
cover ourselves with gold of have-nowt

        So all might know
        what each   however humble
        owes to the state   the poor brought tubes of lice

and a piece of cheese with female worms
macho worms   worms perished
gilt with the gold of have-nowt

        while king-flocks   Sun-flocks
        came in from the highlands
        and the king slept in sheets of vicuña

while the stone came down from the mountains
stopped   weeping tears of blood
weary stone   could go no further

       truth is   while being hauled
       fell from some twenty thousand hands
       crushing three thousand

Clamber this height   you're food for vultures
eagle to buzzard   at royal feet
Noon ringed with blood   ink   smoke

       War breaks in kings   the llaica said
       cult state and law   to perish
       voice unintelligible   so choked with tears

and the king looked up into its eyes
This Sun   turning round without tiring
we may deduce is not alive

       some tethered animal   circling its stake
       a javelin   gone where it's sent
       not where it wants to go

cleaving the sea   drying up water
dives under earth   a clever swimmer
comes up with dawn in its hands

       if it were master of itself   it might stand still
       visit the unknown pastures of the sky
       rest on its way   without necessity

Emeralds to glass   by disbelievers
rain-vase up there   shattered by thunder
brother and sister war   races dismembered

yet pass through gold and silver gardens
into the temple
altars   and mummies

(the Suns go without eating
some give them grain like birds
*frankly I know no*t)

king-mummies   later times
carried by Indians in their arms
to gringos for home-showings

through streets   wrapped in white sheets
Indians kneeling bowing sobbing
face bathed in tears

many gringos too   taking off hats
Indians so touched by this
none could express their feelings

Everything in the world   suddenly changed to gold
fabulous beggars of your own secretions
and gold itself will then be made of gold

He who weeps blood
He who changes the face of the world
She who's as white as an egg

He who told the end in his dreams
He who has not yet come
The Beautiful   called back in dreams

And gold itself will then be made of gold

XV.

"¡Indio después del hombre y antes de el!"

"Ah querer, éste, el mío, éste, el mundial,
interhumano y parroquial, proyecto!"
POEMAS HUMANOS

Declared by Haravec
        Women change men
to what they'd have them be
        never by staying with
but leaving them

Unnecessary now   thread
        self-inheriting
uninterruptedly
        steps unimpaired
reach to the highest altar

power to hold imbibed with her secretions
        milk breasts express
blood on her thighs
        sweat underarm
her running make-up

drunk   drunk with Sun-juice
        Moon-spirit   star-pisco
from all these ducts   ice-cold canals
        height once made clear
plunging from mountains

        Rimac tongue-twisted
            Pachacamac silenced
      belted for once   in the king-city
            bread baked with blood
      Sun   kiss-implored

roads watched
                    for oriflammes
rushing day-sins   out to the suburbs
                    torches   to burn night-sin
out of the soul   cleansed   waiting answers

tribes closing ranks
                    got up   imagine angels
with condor wings   fox   puma skins
                    sardine-anointed
straddling whales

chiefs dragged in triumph
                    naked on litters
relations / drums
                    hands holding batons
to their own bellies

Blood wept enough   conquest played out
                    eyes washed enough   turned to the wall
eyes from which her eyes look out
                    surprised by morning
and his voice   when all speech had been lost

mummies afoot
                    dry skins hydrated   Coya juices
whose hand on his hand turns the world
                    done adulterous days   done partings
bird-song   plain marital

marriage dance woven
                    Pizarro's beard
tweaked to the soulful harp
                    old / young   still younger
back to first brother   first sister

held by the long   long   fingers of the Sun
         nursed in its arms
they cannot fall
        threshold revered
stepping-stone uplifted

            Line free from taint
                step out again   to give the laws
         at Huanacauri   sank first time
               teach men   teach women
         ascension in

                      these ways of light

XVI.

*"No es grato morir, señor, si en la vida nada se deja y
si en la muerte nada es posible, sino sobre lo que pudo
dejarse en la vida"*

*"Y la gallina pone su infinito, uno por uno;
Sale la tierra hermosa de las humeantes sílabas"*
POEMAS HUMANOS

And he passed   around midnight
        from the living land into the living land
        from the one shore to the same shore
        from the mountain to the mountain
saying   do you believe
        saying   do you believe
as she laughed him happy

the nail-heads reached his palms
        how long a time it was
        he saw some heaven   and much more hell
        passed to the selfsame shore
saying   do you believe
        the other shore is there
has no description

while she fussed among children and hens
        fussed among shadows and flowers
        in a garden they'd made of Peru
        with Vallejo's mother's roses
saying   do you believe
        the poet's lost his crown
and brought the breakfast round

at each end of the house   in the Sun's long arms
        windows brood streets
        their curving iron bars
        swans' necks and harps

saying   do you believe
                    we have inheritance
we've taken to this earth

white sheets washed in the lakes   blue sheets in rivers
                    pillowslip on the wind
                    mattress in fire
                    this is the bed of life   beyond description
saying   do you believe
                    the only shore worth knowing
there is no other

and come she said come   into this living room
                    the center of the house
                    the locket of my arms
                    I'll make such brews   as peace is made on
saying   do you believe
                    this angry zeal   this searing love
is our geography

and he took his life   this life   into his hands
                    and made to use it
                    and he saw the laughter brimming in her eyes
                    feared not to lose it
saying   do you believe
                    after all the loves in my life
this is the one

all poems have dissolved into a song   and we survive
                    this poem goes that way
                    cannot go wrong
                    peak climbed   sea swum
saying   do you believe
                    what a crime against the country of our life
nearly committed

and rose again   around   with joyful rising
              setting the world to work
              along their daily rounds
              and taught the ass to bray   and dog to bark
saying   do you believe
              this is a destiny
the Sun is in the sky   and needs no moving

Afterword

These poems were written in Pachichiyut, Lago de Atitlán, Guatemala, without the benefit of any direct knowledge of Inca Tahuantinsuyu or modern Peru. Abroad unexpectedly, I happened to have with me an inexpensive *César Vallejo, sus Obras Poéticas* (Ediciones Perú, Lima, n.d.), as well as a copy of Ernesto More's *Vallejo en la encrucijada del drama Peruano* (Bendezu, Lima, 1968). Among a very few other works, was a copy of Alain Gheerbrandt's edition, in an English version, of *Los Comentarios Reales* by the great half-Inca writer Garcilaso de la Vega (1539–1616): *The Incas* (Maria Jolas translation, Avon Library, New York, 1964).

The poems were begun, in somewhat different form, well before a reading of the material to hand and my first thought had been to entitle them, either after Amerigo, or, more pertinently, after Garcilaso El Inca. As I read Vallejo, concurrently with Garcilaso, the modern poet began to take first place. I greatly felt the lack of Clayton Eshleman's translations but that lack enabled me to treat Vallejo's work on my own terms, with what success it is not for me to judge.

Ultimately, Vallejo's work came to play an active role in the ongoing poems. First, quotations from him in Spanish serve as epigraphs to each poem in the sequence. Second, the poems numbered *A* to *D*, written after the others, are poems about him, using fragments of his verse, more or less loosely adapted by myself without respect to their own original position in the Vallejo corpus. This liberty approximates to treating Vallejo's lines as "found-poetry": I apologize only to his fierce shade. Finally, a few lines appear within the other poems, bleeding out, as it were, from the poems *A* to *D*. It should be added that some of the quotations and adaptations are taken from recorded Statements and letters of Vallejo to be found in More's *"anecdotario"*.

Readers of Garcilaso will have little difficulty in identifying those parts of the sequence which are indebted to him. An exile, like Vallejo, he comes to be identified with the caesar-poet hero of the poems, through the mediumship of the Incas themselves, and primarily Manco Capac, legendary founder of the Royal Line.

Nathaniel Tarn,
Pachichiyut,
September, 1969

II

CHOICES

Scorpions

Black
    diverse sizes
    according to how free the day has been
            of tangible
  trouble

with that property
    unheralded
         brought down by no known movement
      witnessed
        from the ceiling down
             or the floor up
   one streak   and here

   pincers   wrestlers' holds
       tail   curling/uncurling   birthday trumpet
more beautiful than spiders   cleaner
        filleted spine   smoked
              with a speed inside
    would collect rent
          now   pronto

tail through that hand
    nail through that hand
        wood bought when we met
           matured about that time
     head reaching the palm
    about midnight
        and
      that passage of heaven
         that cross of hell
      and

hop
       that other shore
      '
             has no
                 description

like

        I leave you newsless
        I tell you nada
        I give you nothing to go on
        you guess   see

and cry
      don't mind how much
            with my essence   love you deep enough
    (which can afford   housed   husbanded)
           (until I die)

about the speed they take to pass from man to man

    the speed I take

       with a shoe

          at that

                waving
tail

Taking Leave

How do you live
            saying nothing but
      goodbye   whole day
          whole night   quitting one thing
                 after another   taking leave
       everything done   that long affair

                no longer eat this
                    without thoughts
             no longer come across this
                    without thoughts
             no longer think this
                    without further thoughts

frailty of world
       frailty of arches
              trestles   arches
              steps
                    buttresses
  belts   strings   ropes   chains

all that receding
       licks back towards you
   like a leaving tide
           your feet alone on the sand
                nothing but sand
          as far as eye can reach
            nothing but feet

            in rubbish   detritus
               still the trace
         in emptyness   void
               still the trace
         in forgetfulness
               still the trace

and make a song   out of dying
                and make a song   out of the strangled throat
                        like that swan dying
                that stuffed trumpet
                                blaring fuck-it
                unvoiced
                                        singing still

                        and about the city
                                she goes about in
                        what about the city
                                she goes about in
                        streets   corners   shops
                                she goes about in

balancing love   and hate
                saying o.k.   I'll not . . . . . . impediments
        o.k. you take that man   you make that choice
                        at your own level
        o.k. those grapes   sour as all hell
                        nothing but silence does

                length of the silence dearest god

Apparition

If you see a woman
         with the wind around her hair
  color of such and such
                     send her this way
      she might be mine

coming back on buses
           from other villages
  that'll be her on the street
                  at that corner
      or that corner
               patting a dog

and the other hand   out of that window
      and her eyes   in that glass
                her slippers
     running across the street
              empty

her voice coming out of that song
             that radio
  song saying nothing goes
          with that
      you know
sadness

on the wings of a moth
        lower lids salmon
  upper lids chocolate
            eyes on the lowers
  ochre ringed black
           her eye-shadow

breasts in those fruit hanging there
              at two for five
                soon as they reach the basket
    locals will sell
                    look at the nipples
   no mildew   fresh

what she has to tell
         the way she tells it
               with just that cruelty
                    she happens nowadays
                  §to go into
                  whenever she would raise

       question of me

the less she sends her news
      the more
              in that dog's guts
squashed by a passing car
              she plunges hands

Accidents

Is there something to it
        if
  that glass goes out of your hand
            onto the floor   for no known reason
      first time it's carried

and you watch
      in the long year
             it travels
                  to the ground
    and can't recuperate

or
        if on first cooking
     out of solitude
        a sheet of oil leaps from the pan
             blisters that meadow twixt thumb and index

or
        lights go dead in the night
    priorities are lost
           the house key lost in a locked case
        that case key too

and you
        talk to yourself an awful lot
                getting words wrong
        the syntax wrong
              break off just as the
explanation
      begins to make it

more in the evening than in the morning
      telling yourself bad times are just the chores

                    running the house of silence
          returns you to
                              and even
          not what happens / but reactions to it

matter the most
                              while
          one
              clean
                    silent
                          knife
                              pares flesh from bone

leaving the spine to stand

                    a blasted tree

          and the suffering   is so quiet

Choices

As if to keep
        two houses standing
   at the selfsame time
                were anything a man could do
     for any length of time

and let this flower its own way
        and that too
   give them their independence
            balk at no insult
                balk at no gossip

that figure
        with two heads
   perhaps hermaphrodite
           more weird than beautiful
                torn down the central eye
     river of blood

yet I am one
        and they each   one
   but in different places
           they'll never conjugate
    those rivers
           between the gates

and if I
     like sucking blood
              that time of month
      where salt is the usual portion
           as the old man who wrote the Witch
      did to his glory

is it not
      because it touches sea
  with rhyming tides
         because it dies
  with rhyming tides
           and the gates let you in

but this is it
      to know which blood I'll drink
  which rhythm follow
         the blood I've fertilized
  the blood I've left to cool
             too long
   till it's gone mad

and a little sour
     in its black hair
        a little bitch
   in its surface features
        technically insane

telling the world
     for what it's worth
      it's moving out on me
    till I can't find it
         in the tar
     the pitch
       it has hardened to

Swimmer

As I kick off
          below firs   below grass
                    below mocking birds
     head down into the lake
                                        masked
               skimming the undertow
          of our achievements

with a head
               bad for heights and depths
          so when abysses pass
                         threaded by fish
               razors and knives
                              I can imagine
                    these are the mirrors of disaster

I lose your shadow
                    body's consistency offset
          by fears of loss of loss
                    absence of spring in my loins
               lock in your crotch will not give way
                                   the molten lake
               worked by my heart   like the first waters

in this the season of the dead
               albeit bright with gold as at creation
                    albeit mountains shine as if well-tempered
          and the limbs of valleys gleam resplendent
                         flowers of every shape and size
                              but always yellow
                         bloom for the dead
                    shimmer above the waters
          like the first suns

here I travel
       among the silences
               among the voices
      here I do
    without the worry about the doing
      here I master
with a sweetness of knowledge no other knows

I find your ghost
       in the deepest trough
             clothed in her mail
     in the deepest caves
  with crabs and their scissor ways
             with whitebait homing
   and the wires of the fish of the sea

and the noonday sun
      nails my head into the water
           with a golden stroke

For Buffy Sante-Marie

Suddenly
        she
              looks
         a thousand years old
      with just that violence
            kick of the wind
               her leg gives sideways
     her grin breaking from tanned
          drum of her face
    taut nose
body half-bent
        lance   jack-knife
howl in the voice
      as if the stars had grown violent
         suddenly   on an impulse

   then
quick as hawk from throne
          or wren from hiding
            or still small wind of summer
     in the nostrils of the dead
           her confidence
      friendship in ghostly eyes
         blue of cut turquoise
no
   well of sweet water
         no
           fish blood
    from a very old
        very old
           sea

black bear comes out of a sigh
                    cloud as small as a paw
           on the horizon
                              it is the distance
              not the white   not the law
                         not the treaty
     not the ghosts who walk out of battle
             with noses to the ground
        but the walls
             more dangerous than stone
          thin as paper
             meeting back to back
             the trackless wastes
          so distanced from each other that they meet
                              now back to back

bears
        mountain-lions
                    death   in their paws
           in their embraces
                         bigger than we have been

it is November in the month of the dead
     and the dust begins to rise a little from the roads
              omen of distant summer
       it is as if the dead   blew on the roads
                    when the rains are over
           as they walk by   looking down hill
                       and the dust responds a little

she stomps in this country
                    and everyone goes native now
                              out to the streets
        with the smell of our fear on the wind

perhaps   we will all get killed soon

Ageing Hands

You will not lay your hands on
                                    any of this
            no   it eludes you
      however hands
                        will start from this
                              seizing every limb of your life
      you'll suffer change
                  as if you had been rolled
         a lengthy age
                        the kind of age the buddhas talk about
      in an icy sea

the defect
            so near invisible no one will ever guess
      those barrens
                        not mind's defect
                                    not will's
                        falter at gate   break at alternative
                              not signal point of character
      neon in darkness   falling
                        the terrible loss you suffer
      condemned to death
                        out of all proportion

but the small smell on your breath
                        the wrinkle of skin at your neck
      base of the neck
                        that dagger patch
      the white hair in an unlikely place
                              on the hidden body

            and
                  between thumb and finger
                                    a little desert
                  the cracks of small plots
      parched by the sun

behind the coping with every day
        the task well done   the flawless execution
  yes   that murder of everything in the well-doing
       gasp for breath
the person who cries in the night
         who has terrible dreams he does not remember
         or remembers for a moment unwillingly
   whose life is done
                whose future lies condemned
           like a drowning canyon

never knowing   never guessing what brought him down

the hands
    hands caressed youth once
                into other hands
      that knew once how to be wings
          how to jump off trees
            and land safely
         how to break falls for others
           cups for all agonies
          cups   chalices
      fields of bright wisdom

ageing   burnt out like dying stars   uncapturing

The Great Odor of Summer

The Great Odor of Summer

The land has been dead in its pores   all the war long
now wakes to dogwood   without transition
we've had no time at all for spring
great perfume exhalations on the edges of summer
fast water births and blood-filled afterbirths
the gloat of trees   leaf legions shining
trash of bird squadrons   animal regiments
coursing of eagles through clouds   freeing the perfumes
needles of warbler beaks in the clouds opening avenues
              for the freshening rain

        High on sleep   high on our own desires
              to the high scream of jays   their presages
        taking over these fields from the predators
              our own authority returning to our hands
        high on sleep   high over arguments
              messages   codes   informations
        listening to the say-so of time
              South Carolina talking the other day
        of the line which is the circle which is the line
              while more inches than needed were to lie down in Ohio

and in the trees the leaves were opening to a music
        not only the trees were to hear
seeds were preparing their shadows
        not only for generations of birds
and warblers were weaving round thick trunks
        a female lure to our preparations
              to perfume the reddening rain

        In a small corner of the dreamtime
              I dreamed the ceremony I had not seen on the first field
        those many years ago in the abundance of waters
              it was the pendant rite of bringing in the summer

ah the rain   we had talked of that   had practiced that
                    except that here the colors were as bright
as hay and corn and cardinals
and the brown of an infant's shit
            the war-chief had looked up at me sideways
                    my presence worried him
            and the peace-chief too   holding his kite
                    with which he was about to tie the earth
        to outer suns   to stars
they decided to carry out the rites
                            just as I woke
        in a corner of the dream
                                between hut and hut

and in her thickets   in her lowest reaches
where revolution slips   in her red placenta
we look to find in the bent over branches
                the paradisal forking of desire
these odors of her effluence   her loving pollution
love's yielding form as yet unknown
                    to all our lunge and parry in the dark

        I came to poetry late
                had looked to other things for my family
        and woke to find myself an orphan to all else
                    then came my mother-fathers
            brothers   sisters   cousins
    sons   daughters   grandchildren   as thick as sand
        in the shape of other poets
        whose books I kissed
                as precisely as I would kiss a stone
        on falling in love with its polish

Warblers' wings like mouths brushing against the dark
butterflies panting   wet cunts of violets
        worms in the slime of the moon
the sun's hair streaming
            bent to our roots as our heads batter the skies

the great odor of love spreads from our crotches out there
                    to break the gathering dark

        Well
                    What will you do with the Academy?
                    saw down the branch you sit on?
                    change it?   burn it?   rape it?
                    drown it in wine and sperm?
                    dance it to ritual?
                    retrieve it for disaster?
                    fruitful disaster?
                    take it over for your own harvest?
                    occupy the great odor?

When we sit down to talk of values
        and start where most men end
neglecting the simple beginnings
        we make an end of the Academy
I am interested in those who begin at the beginnings
philosophers in caves   playing with light and shadow
taking the explanations of others who sit in caves
        and welding them together into one answer
            Look do you know
that 99% of mankind is syncretistic
        that isms are a luxury of the rich
and that we
            with our eyes of ice
            our eyes of petal and flame
            our eyelids like the wings of summer flies
                in the great light of total opposition
are poor   and rightly poor   and rightly   rightly   poor?

        And Beatrice · if she had lived
                    what then?
            if she'd been met with   at every corner
                        by the poet at his work
            or at his meditations

if she had walked with that sweet front of hers to the wind
  like an ageing revolution with banners
her hair against the sharp horizon of her wings
  with rhetoric on her upper lip
  and the booty of war on the lower?

No   the muse dies
    to the high cry of jays
the muse ages
        she changes altogether
            the muse dies
        to the high omen of jays in the cut-up of the summer sky
            and we start another revolution
            our authority returns to us
            in the great odor of summer
            in the freshness of our own days

The small blue world in my hand
            like an eye I have lost
I glare at with the other eye
            the small blue world
running with blood   prepared for you
    while we select the America we are dreaming
and the great elegy that the world is writing for itself
            in silence somewhere
    hardly known to itself
which we recite behind our voices   each time we speak

To the Academy in the tundra   to the Academy in the forest
to the Academy in the fields   to the Academy in the marshes
to the Academy in the mountains   to the Academy in the clouds
to the Academy in the rivers   to the Academy in the seas
to the Academy of love   to the Academy of pleasure
to the Academy of beauty   to the Academy of desire
to the Academy of surprise   to the Academy of imagination

to the blood on the pavements   and on the bayonets
to the blood on the brain's gutters   on the heart's highways
to the blood on our hands   and in our armpits
to the blood in our eyes   and in our matted hair
to the blood over this field as over Ohio
we subscribe   high on sleep   high on our own desires
     under the screams of jays   in the great odor of summer

v. v. mcmlxx

III

OCTOBER

A sequence of ten poems
followed by
Requiem Pro Duabus Filiis Israel

The Curtains

The leaves are coming down
the walls of my life
    are not more solid

I hear the leaves coming down
at night they make the noise of footsteps
or the kisses of children
they fall like a curtain
    between the leaves
bits of a sky we try to remember

"There was in that man
had he been left unshaken by his stars
    a happy disposition"

On the other side of the curtain
the fathomless country lies about us
the farms
    sitting like loaves among the fields
the animals
    at home in their own breaths
needing no byres
    and birds never a roost

We have seen it
  we know it by heart
    men of no season

I shall build on nothing
on nothing build my house
out of the iron nail remorselessly
hammered into the ground of this dead year
the nail so bald so cold
out of humiliation and the grinding feet
on nothing build my house

and when the leaves are fallen
and hammering is done
the curtains of the house will have been hung

Through which we glimpse
the place we shall inhabit
                    full void   that memory

The Pictures

Certain Octobers
ran with blood
as if the sun had touched the earth
and turned its rivers to blood
ours is a quiet time needing to build

I had never been a young poet
those dreams of entering a room   smiling
turning the head this way and that   bowing
taking a perfumed hand
leading the most beautiful away to the waltz

"You have an openness around the eyes
that shows a willingness to learn and to accept
the new experience   with this you cannot age"

The pictures dream in an empty hall
the figures in the pictures dream
their heads thrown back   with throats exposed
to knives of light   a ceiling falling
our hesitations touch each other

I dream they are calling me
the young faces eager for what I have to say
I've not yet found the way to say it

Our shoulders rub together
we sketch the desire inside us with our hands
we are given
moments   a succession of moments
when shall we get
                         time we ask
uninterrupted time
and still more time when conversation fails

exhausted talk drifting away from our mouths
like mist

                         and perhaps sleep
the satisfaction of silence

There should be
a society for the protection of
the deeply married

The Screens

Over the park   a play of mist
hiding this lawn then that
on lacquered screens   a coat of clouds

dew at mid-day
covers the grass as far as I can see
the blackbirds drowning in the dew

Death spreads itself over the silver carpet
I die it here   I die it there
the pebbles break under my feet

Parts of my life as clear
as hands I hold before me
parts dark   yielding no residue

Sane and insane
progressing side by side   the light may laugh
the dark seethes like a pit

Dog-worries shake
the business of the day
from trees that have no hands to hide

I am about to bark
birds scatter quick
a stag stands frozen in his lacquered cage

Something must break

The Dark Night

Perhaps the most terrible thing about la noche oscura
is that it comes about in broad daylight

My life has moved out of me and taken possession
of territories I have not mapped
I walk by myself   empty and wondering
where this or that has been misplaced

If once I wanted to lay the world
and all my salvages
at somebody's feet
that desire is now done with

Someone must return all I've lost to me
and feed me to my prime
I shall be rich and give away treasure
allowed to proceed another few years

Not so long ago I marched through London
for something better than we have
though the details elude me
There was some question in my mind
of rediscovering a fire   some youth
some fire for myself would also cease to burn
children I did not love but others loved as I
can sometimes love my children

and London was littered with banners
black and red flags   the writing on the wall
the ashes of old fires we carry in ourselves
we covered much asphalt and green grass

Above our heads   in a misted sky
the shape of branches made a trellis against the sun
"—somewhere there is a country where no leaves fall—"
consumed in its own light

and on the branches   birds of paradise
spun like raucous fireworks with long tail feathers
in a world we had never reached   any of us
in a light we had never seen burning

The Music

We lie   and listen to the music in our sleep
and trees outside touch leaves
and through their thicknesses the fast birds weave
and Mozart's angels weave   and not one space

remains between the music   angels   flight   or sleep

If   as I'd not believed   all these long years
it really is once only   life just once only
no one can justify   a single life

and to be a sparrow among eagles
takes a great deal of time
and a great deal of being a sparrow

Here and there among layers
a single leaf torments itself in the wind
beats like a wing   throbs like an instrument
the players reach an end   leave one by one

                              we wonder at the fall

your head is falling   asleep between my hands

The Words

The ground   takes all the leaves
in autumn's gift
and raises other trees for other seasons

Those who are going down into themselves
on every page of every newspaper
seeping away under our sullen noses

their catalog should be as bare
as autumn trees
the names saying no more
no less than branches

We have not blood enough
to agonize with Viets
another day Biafrans
another day the Czechs

the lovely tribes   falling like shadows

If we must play with words
the nouns should be like lungs
sooted with smoke
the verbs like cancers   ravaging the blood

Where is the life I lead
how dare I lead it
how shall the earth survive
endless attrition

the flies are falling from the leaves
our words will soon be pared
to a single sound

The Field of Merit

I didn't know where to cast my seed
all these months
but the field is fallow again

the field has returned from the moon
refreshed from its long disuse
free of broiling creatures

I sow my death there
and get a fertile chemistry
sweet oils of grazing

brushing the leaves away
with a moist hand
the hand of mist   the hand of rain

the earth is wet to the touch
its fine black hairs
curl round my fingers beckoning

Come night I shall have grazed
a crater like the moon's
a deep   inverted pregnancy

the field is filleted
down to the arching spine
and every lip I speak with

and every answering lip
drooling loam songs
shines with its uncontrollable brown dews

The Joining of Hands

Our hands   unable to touch
our fingers begin to think
we work across landscapes
          thick with impediments
I begin to walk through you
          you walk through me for a while
coming upon clear prairies
          and then we are retrieved

Sleepwalking in the streets
crossing a bridge
as if we were to couple
          among the roots of trees
I've laid our freedom on this town
          a map   a grid
and the sea has rushed in
          to drown intelligence

In the poem I give you my hands
where you will sense
their joining overhead
          give me the birds of summer
beyond intelligence
          for they know ways in air
far countries where we need not meet
          married already there

In the poem I give you my hands

          you cannot lose

The Residue

For the unspoken
for what will not be said
because   at this moment of time
no words exist

For the way we meet
the sleeping partnership
the lyric on the brink
of failing recognition

the silence in me when you turn to sleep
the dream I cannot interrupt
where you are meeting me
and I run

There will be words tomorrow
there is always a little left
that is the state of grace
the state of poetry

and when you know there is no end
the end is near
the fountain's drying up
the ice is glittering

Yet I preserve the river
flooding both grass and stars
where the meridian cleaves
your breath in two

the ore melts in the leaves
the grass under their gold
is green as a working hand
on the paper of morning

The Silence

I am a silent place
yes   look   I have done it now
the birds migrate through me
the leaves peel off my bones
the seasons drop their privacies
            undress through me

I am a listening place for your ears
where you can hear the sea as in a shell
            and all its languages
now there is an island in the sea
now there are birds on the trees
            the falling leaves reveal the birds

I flow through this town   the traffic flows
round my escarpments   my retreat
I am the guest of this town
it is feeding me
limbs   smiles   a thousand faces
            I talk to none of them

and yet   where the birds fly
out of my cast-off clothes
where I dare and am dared in the silence
there is never more than a breath
to draw between gain and loss
            yes   of all the world

and he approaches me
the sinner of a moment ago
his mouth thick with a swarm of flies

but the birds are free of vermin
flying through me
and the carpet of leaves is clean

Requiem Pro
Duabus Filiis Israel

Requiem Pro Duabus Filiis Israel

to A & S

...et perducant te in civitatem sanctam Jerusalem.
Chorus angelorum te suspiciat et cum Lazare quondam
paupere aeternam habeas requiem.
Requiem aeternam dona eis, Domine: et lux perpetua luceat eis.

The trees proffer their leaves
                        she is not here
the birds prepare to mate
                        she keeps no company
the roads are bright with traffic festivals
the wings of windows laze on singing air
the earth ages another day
                        another day
                                another day

she will not age
                                she does not see it
she is not witness to

                        this celebration

and our days have died   there is no energy
in hand or foot   the brain is dull
thought starved before it comes to birth
the dream locked in our minds   tedium destroying
                                all our occasions

Some weary angel took its eyes off her
turning its pinions from a faded sun
one moment
                                and she side-slipped to
silence   and speechlessness.

Ruth in reverse
Boaz asleep under so many trees
after his work in many different fields
she was confused   wanting to follow
into closed regions he would not allow
into his languages
whose syllables were dark   whose phrases   dark
destroyed the very messages they carried her
his myth not hers   nor could it ever be
while unbeknown to her   all ships had foundered
all harbours drained into the sea
all trace of any home she could have had
erased from memory

With lungs still full of gas
with nostrils bruised by her last breath
she lies oak-packaged on a pedestal
beside her   in white cloth
the child she took into the oven with her
after the crude excitement
the unexpected scandal
that was not done to call for any poem
now all her parts
committed to the fire
her crown of hair   first   and her hidden hair
under her arms   and hair between her thighs
and hair along the limbs   since she was dark
born of a foreign sun   and then the flesh
the hard flesh of the hands   the silk of inner limbs
down through the muscle   melting   down the reluctant bone
past a small yelp of soul   the sob of spirit
to the still ash   transmuted excrement

Now those are busy who will set her down
that language might survive
now some write literary history
some see her snared in myth

also themselves   the good she does for them
some write their in memoriams
and I this requiem
whose tongue could then have summoned   had I been so required
the hiss and vowel of her family

Daughter of daughter in the founding line
these daughters of the people gone   confused
the alien language squatting on our tongues
while from the coffin her clear cry for help
participation   and a place to sleep
in death's white syllables goes misunderstood
we give her up now   to the lapping fire
to Terezin   Auschwitz   and Buchenwald
for laziness   for emptiness of spirit

As tight as love   in the first days of love
romance unlived with her   as tight as love
the mind so tight   no other thought can slip
into the tight circumference
                              the moment blasted
each moment blasted in the thought of her
                              firstborn among the dead
when we no longer find the time to die
and   soon   will never need to

Beyond all blessings   hymns   praises   and consolations
that may be uttered in this world again
and say   Amen

Oseh shalom bim'romov
Hu ya-aseh shalom
oleinu v'al kol Yisroeil
v'imru Omein

V'imru Omein

A Note from the Publisher

This volume is part of a series that is devoted to recovering out-of-print volumes that – in my view – should be made available again. The books date from the 1970s to the 2000s and all of the volumes published so far have been of some importance to me in one way or another. Most are long out of print, although some can be found within subsequent collected editions.

A Nowhere for Vallejo was published in the UK after the author's emigration to the USA, and it appeared a few months after the volume's US publication. The title sequence is, in my view, a major work and one which is very much a harbinger of things to come in the author's work. *October* had already appeared in a typically finely-produced edition from Asa Benveniste's London-based Trigram Press in 1969. Attentive readers will note that the use of American or British spelling is a little erratic in the volume as a whole, as befits a poet who straddled the Atlantic; we have left the original spelling choices as they were and have simply corrected a few minor typos, more often in the Spanish epigraphs than elsewhere.

Tony Frazer
July 2023

Printed in July 2023
by Rotomail Italia S.p.A., Vignate (MI) - Italy